A NOTE TO PARENTS

Reading Aloud with Your Child

Research shows that reading books aloud is the single most valuable support parents can provide in helping children learn to read.

- Be a ham! The more enthusiasm you display, the more your child will enjoy the book.
- Run your finger underneath the words as you read to signal that the print carries the story.
- Leave time for examining the illustrations more closely; encourage your child to find things in the pictures.
- Invite your youngster to join in whenever there's a repeated phrase in the text.
- Link up events in the book with similar events in your child's life.
- If your child asks a question, stop and answer it. The book can be a means to learning more about your child's thoughts.

Listening to Your Child Read Aloud

The support of your attention and praise is absolutely crucial to your child's continuing efforts to learn to read.

- If your child is learning to read and asks for a word, give it immediately so that the meaning of the story is not interrupted. DO NOT ask your child to sound out the word.
- On the other hand, if your child initiates the act of sounding out, don't intervene.
- If your child is reading along and makes what is called a miscue, listen for the sense of the miscue. If the word "road" is substituted for the word "street," for instance, no meaning is lost. Don't stop the reading for a correction.
- If the miscue makes no sense (for example, "horse" for "house"), ask your child to reread the sentence because you're not sure you understand what's just been read.
- Above all else, enjoy your child's growing command of print and make sure you give lots of praise. *You are your child's first teacher—and the most important one. Praise from you is critical for further risk-taking and learning.*

—Priscilla Lynch
Ph.D., New York University
Educational Consultant

For Kellan
—F.M.

For Brian and Emily
—L.S.

A Note to the Reader:

Manatees are endangered animals and they are protected by laws. The author, Faith McNulty, and her friend Woody, a biologist, received special permission to approach the manatees.

Although this is a true story, the illustrator, drawing from her imagination, has depicted Faith as a young girl. At the time of the story, Faith was already a grown woman.

The Editor

Text copyright © 1994 by Faith McNulty.
Illustrations copyright © 1994 by Lena Shiffman.
All rights reserved. Published by Scholastic Inc.
CARTWHEEL BOOKS® and HELLO READER!® are registered trademarks of Scholastic Inc.

Library of Congress Cataloging-in-Publication Data

McNulty, Faith.
    Dancing with manatees / by Faith McNulty ; illustrated by Lena Shiffman.
        p.   cm. — (Hello reader! Level 4)
    Summary: Examines the physical characteristics, behavior, and evolution of this gentle creature.
    ISBN 0-590-46401-9
    1. Manatees—Juvenile literature. [1. Manatees.] I. Shiffman, Lena, ill. II. Title. III. Series.
QL737.S63M38   1994
599.5'5—dc20   93-7593
                                                      CIP
                                                      AC

12   11   10   9   8   7   6   5   4   4   5   6   7   8   9/0
                    Printed in the U.S.A.   23
            First Scholastic printing, April 1994

Dancing with
Manatees

by Faith McNulty
Illustrated by Lena Shiffman

Hello Reader!—Level 4

SCHOLASTIC INC.
New York   Toronto   London   Auckland   Sydney

Once I swam in clear water
in a wide river.
I held my breath and looked down.
Swimming underwater
I could see through my mask —
white sand below me, weeds swaying,
a tin can gleaming, little fish darting,
and my friend Woody swimming
in his dark rubber suit.

I came up to breathe.
Woody popped up near me.
He took off his mask.
"Did you find one?" I asked.
"Over there." He pointed.
"By the raft.
Alice is taking a nap."
I swam toward the raft.
Fins made swimming easy.

I dove down into the water and there was Alice —
a great, gray creature
with a soft, round, rubbery look,
resting quietly on the sandy bottom.
Her face was round and wrinkled.
Her front flippers were like
short, blunt arms.
Her tail was like a Ping-Pong paddle.
She looked like a huge toy balloon.
She was a manatee,
an animal that lives in water
and breathes air.

Woody had named her Alice.

While I watched, she opened a small eye.

She turned her head and looked at me.

Her flippers waved gently.

She opened her mouth.

Silver bubbles popped out.

Alice had burped.

I swam up to the sunny surface
to breathe.
Woody was on the raft.
I sat beside him, and we talked
about manatees.
Woody is a biologist.
He was studying the manatees
that visit rivers and bays
along the coast of Florida.
Once there were thousands
of Florida manatees.
Now there are only a few hundred.
By studying them, Woody hopes
we can find ways
to help them survive.
Here are some things he told me.

Manatees live in water all their lives.
Long ago — millions of years ago — their ancestors
lived on land and ate grass.
Little by little, they began to go
into the water,
perhaps to find food there
or to escape enemies by swimming.
In the water, they didn't need legs and feet.
Their front legs evolved into flippers.
Manatees still have toenails
where front toes used to be.
Their hind legs evolved into a paddle-shaped tail.

The shape of their bodies also changed.
It became smooth and tapered to slide
easily through the water, and padded with fat
to keep them warm.
Their outer ears disappeared.
Manatees have only a tiny hole
where outer ears used to be.
Even so, they can hear very well.

When they are underwater
their nostrils close tight and stay shut
until they rise to the surface for air.
They usually breathe every four minutes.
When they sleep, they come up for a breath
every ten minutes.
The ancestors of manatees were mammals.
They fed their babies on milk.
Manatees still do.
A mother manatee has two nipples
on her chest where her baby suckles.

* * *

It is not easy for a scientist to study manatees
because manatees hardly ever show themselves
above water.
Woody spent days and days swimming with them
to learn the secrets of their lives.
He got to know some of them and gave them names.
Alice, Jane, Nelly, Laura, Gertrude,
Jim, and George were his favorites.
Nelly had a baby called Nifty,
and Laura had Laurette.
Laurette had a problem.

A piece of fishing line
was tangled around her tail
and was cutting into her skin.
Woody had tried to pull it off,
but Laurette was scared.

Each time he tried to free her, she slipped away.
Now he was going to try to cut the line off,
but first he had to find her again.

I asked Woody how he could tell
which manatee was which.
"That's the sad part," he said.
"Motorboats run over them.
Sharp propellers cut them and leave scars
on their bodies.
I know them by the scars."
Woody found that each manatee
has its own personality;
some are shy and timid,
some not at all afraid
but full of curiosity and play.

Some seemed to like his company
and let him stroke them.
Manatees like to be touched.
They scratch themselves with their flippers,
rub each other, and bounce off each other
like living beach balls.

While we were talking on the raft
the sun had warmed us.
Woody slipped into the water, and I followed.
Crystal River, where we were swimming,
is perfect for watching manatees.
Warm water bubbles up from a giant spring
and makes a lake that narrows into a river
flowing to the Gulf of Mexico,
seven miles away.

Manatees need warmth.
In cold weather they leave the seashore,
swim up the river, and gather at the warm spring.
In warm weather they go down the river and
scatter in search of the water grasses
on which they graze.
Though they have lived in water
for millions of years, manatees still eat
the way horses do,
using their rubbery upper lips
to pull grass into their mouths,
then biting it off with their teeth.

I saw Woody swim to the center
of the spring and look down,
breathing through his snorkle.
I followed. Woody dove.
Floating face down, I watched
a slow dance underwater
as Woody and a manatee swam in circles
around each other.
The manatee stopped and hung still
in the water staring at Woody
with a look of simple curiosity.
Then it moved and
reached out its flippers
as though to hug him.
It pressed its nose to his mask,
kissing it with its bristly snout.
Woody stroked its huge back
and, as the manatee turned over,
he rubbed its chin and round belly.
Suddenly the dance was over.
The manatee flapped its great paddle tail
and shot off, out of sight.

Back at the raft Woody explained the "kiss."
Manatees use a mixture of smell and taste
the way land animals use smell alone.
Manatees often seem to kiss each other.
They are probably doing
what land animals do
when they touch noses —
getting and giving a message.
The manatee wasn't kissing Woody.
It was wondering who he was.
Manatees have scent glands
under their chins, forelegs, and tail.
They rub these on logs or stones,
leaving a scent message for other manatees.
A scent message might say,
"Hi, there, whoever you are.
Sorry I missed you. See you later."

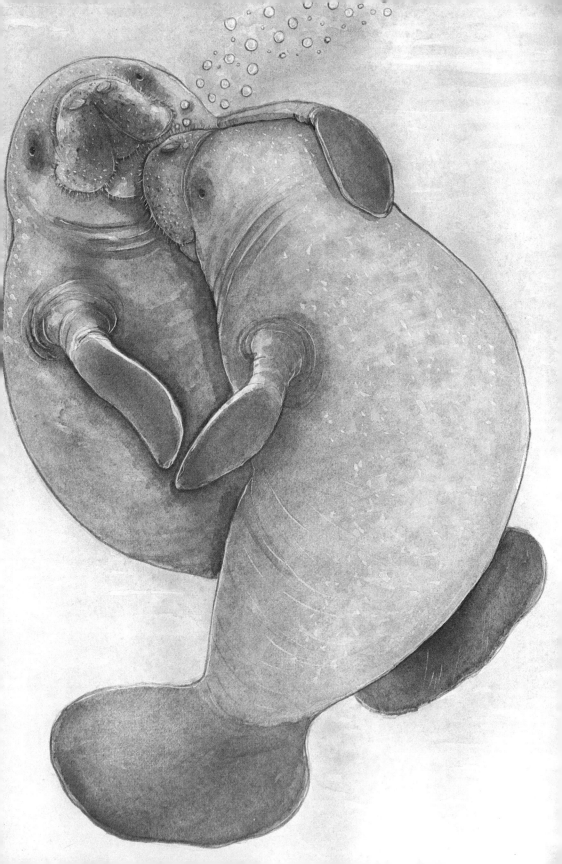

Males and females live separate lives,
except at mating time.
Males check scent posts hoping they will find
the scent of a female that is ready to mate.
When that happens, all the males
in the neighborhood gather around her,
following her wherever she goes.
She leads them all in a merry dance,
twisting and turning to get away.
The males chase her with squeals and grunts.
They give her no peace,
until at last she decides to mate.

One year and one month later a baby is born.
It is born underwater and swims
to the surface for its first breath.
It makes squeaky sounds, and its mother answers.
If it is frightened, it screams.
Mother and baby know each other's voices
and constantly "talk."
The baby follows its mother closely
for two years.
When she sleeps, the baby sleeps
resting on her back.

As it grows older, the young manatee
plays with other youngsters.
They bump and chase and play tag.
They like toys.
Woody told me he saw a manatee
carrying a bottle in its mouth,
another rolling a can on the sandy bottom.
They are curious about any new object.
They have nibbled his flippers,
munched on his anchor rope,
and tried to carry off
his underwater thermometer.

* * *

Later that day Woody and I found
Laura and Laurette.
They were grazing near the shore.
I could see the fishing line
cutting into Laurette's flesh.
Mother and baby stared at us as we swam near.
Suddenly Laura flapped her tail.
She and Laurette disappeared in a cloud
of swirling sand.

Half an hour later, we found them again.
This time, Woody said,
he would try to get behind Laurette
while I stayed in front,
keeping Laura's attention.

I swam slowly toward them.

When the manatees stopped eating

and looked at me, I stayed still,

slowly waving my flippered feet.

They stared at me curiously.

Slowly, gently,

Woody swam closer to Laurette.

He took a knife from his belt.

Slowly, gently,

he reached out and cut.

The nasty, tangled fishing line fell away.

Laurette flapped her tail.
Again we were lost in clouds
of stirred-up silt and sand.
But we felt too happy to mind.

We climbed up on the raft, laughing in triumph.
I asked Woody if he had been afraid
that Laura might attack him.
He shook his head.

Manatees never fight, he said,

even to protect their young.

They have no weapons; no sharp teeth or claws.

They may feel fear, but not anger.

They never hurt each other or any other creature.

They have no enemies except those people

who crowd their rivers and bays with speeding boats,

use clear water as a wastebasket for trash,

and ruin grassy banks with docks and buildings.

But there are other people, like Woody,
who love manatees and do what they can
to keep them safe to lead simple, harmless lives
in their beautiful, watery world.